Once Upon an Accommodation

By
Nina G

Illustrated by
Mean Dave

A Book About Learning Disabilities

Once Upon an Accommodation

By Nina G

Illustrated by Mean Dave

2nd Edition

Preface

According to the Centers for Disease Control and Prevention, nearly 8% of children between the ages of 3 and 17 have Learning Disabilities. Learning Disabilities affect people of all socio-economic levels, ethnicities, genders, and ages. People with Learning Disabilities are faced with many challenges throughout childhood and adulthood. One of the first places they experience difficulties is in school. School is not only an important time to learn academic skills, but also an important time for children with disabilities to learn about their strengths and how to advocate for their rights. Research on successful adults with Learning Disabilities demonstrates that factors associated with these adults include self-awareness, being proactive, perseverance, goal setting, support systems, and emotional coping strategies (www.Frostig.org). Fostering these qualities in children can be just as important as fostering their academic growth.

Once Upon An Accommodation addresses questions children and adults may have about Learning Disabilities, accommodations, and how to go about self-advocacy. These issues are the same whether you are 8 or 88.

The story depicts the main character, Matt, getting accommodations through a 504 meeting/plan. Many children and adults receive accommodations under a 504 plan. Some children may also have an Individualized Education Plan (IEP), but the IEP expires when they exit high school. A 504 plan with appropriate documentation, however, can extend into college. In that vein, college students recently diagnosed with a Learning Disability may also enjoy and benefit from the information in this book.

It is important for individuals with Learning Disabilities to take ownership of their challenges, strengths, and to advocate!

Some suggested possible uses for this book:

- Psychologists might recommend this book to children, adults, and families whom they diagnose with Learning Disabilities or see in therapy.

- Resource Rooms in Special Education Departments or schools specializing in Learning and Attentional Disabilities might carry copies of this book to help students understand and advocate for their particular learning needs.

- Mainstream schools might incorporate this book into their collections to help children with or without disabilities become more attuned to issues surrounding diversity and the disabled community.

- Doctor's offices, psychology/speech/learning clinics, and other practices might display this book in their waiting rooms.

- Parents might read this book with their disabled children to better understand the child's experience. The workbook at the end of the story offers ways for children to express

their own experiences with Learning
Disabilities as well. The activities in "Once
Upon a Workbook" are designed to foster
dialogue and address feelings of isolation that
people with disabilities sometimes experience.

For more resources on Learning Disabilities, become
a fan of Once Upon An Accommodation on Facebook at:
Facebook.com/OnceUponAnAccommodation.

This is Matt. Matt found out that he has a Learning Disability and needs accommodations, but what does that mean?

(Matt)

Matt met Dr. Jerry, the nice psychologist who gave him hours and hours of testing. He explained to Matt what a Learning Disability is. "Some people learn and even think differently from other people," explained Dr. Jerry. "They are just as smart, but they need to do things in a different way."

Dr. Jerry was very excited about the different ways people are smart! He explained to Matt, "People may learn better by seeing, touching, doing, or even singing and rapping! Sometimes interpretive dance may be the best way for them to learn. Once people are taught through the method that works best for them, they get it! And sometimes they even learn it better than people without Learning Disabilities."

Matt thought about all the things he was good at—like sports, playing guitar, and making friends. He was also good at math, but sometimes he got the numbers confused because he needed extra time to really think out the problem he was answering.

Dr. Jerry told Matt that some people have Learning Disabilities, which means their brain is wired differently than other people's brains.

Learning Disabilities can affect people in lots of different ways. For Matt, it meant that he read slower compared to other students in his class.

He also had a difficult time understanding what people said, especially if they spoke really fast or without a lot of feeling in their voice.

He sometimes even confused which was his left and right side. Sometimes people who have these difficulties say they have a Learning Disability called dyslexia.

Dr. Jerry told Matt, "Sometimes when you have a Learning Disability you need accommodations to show what you know and what you can do. An example of an accommodation for someone who uses a wheelchair is a ramp, kind of like the one you used to come into my office. If a person uses a wheelchair, that ramp can get them into the building to do whatever they need to do."

"Because you have a Learning Disability, you won't need a physical ramp, but you will need learning ramps to help you learn."

Matt left Dr. Jerry's office feeling a little bit better, but he was still really confused about what an accommodation was. Since he was so good at research on the Internet, he looked a few things up. This is what he found.

In the 1970s a civil rights law was passed called the Rehabilitation Act. Most civil rights laws protect people because of their race, religion, gender, or because of who they love. But what made the Rehabilitation Act extra cool was that it said people with disabilities had to be treated like everyone else and they could get accommodations. Accommodations were meant to make things more equal for people with disabilities. A lot of activists worked really hard for people like Matt to get accommodations in school.

An accommodation means different things for
different people depending on their disability:

If someone were Deaf and communicated in American
Sign Language, then they could have an interpreter
in class with them.

If someone were blind and could not read the same print as everyone else, then they could get their school books in Braille or on the computer. That way the computer reads it out loud. Books read by the computer are also something that some people with Learning Disabilities and ADHD use. ADHD stands for Attention Deficit Hyperactivity Disorder. People with ADHD sometimes have a hard time focusing on one thing at a time because they're interested in so many things.

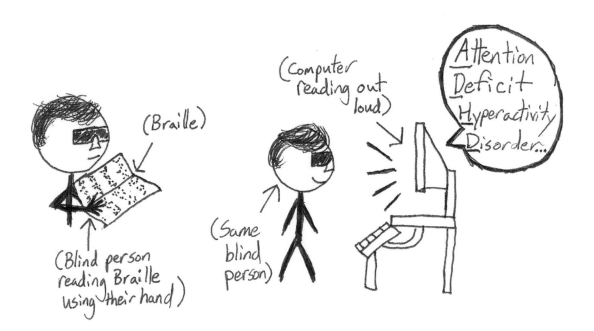

Matt thought to himself,

"So an accommodation doesn't mean that you get something more, it just lets you show what you already know or can do."

Matt found out that he could even get an accommodation at work when he started a new job.

Matt then thought about what sorts of things could or could not be considered an accommodation.

These things were not accommodations:

- Having a straight-A kid in your class do your homework.

- Getting an A for just showing up.

- Getting to fart on the school bully because he made fun of you on Facebook.

- Taking your math quiz while wearing underwear on your head (because you're a smarty-pants).

Some people get the same accommodation whether they are in elementary, high school, or even college.

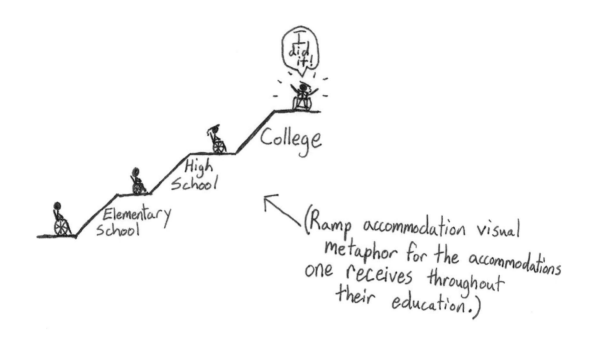

For someone with a Learning Disability, accommodations might include extra time on a test, a private room to take a test, extensions on assignments, taking tests on a computer, and getting books on the computer (so the computer can read the book out loud using text-to-speech). What kind of accommodation a person gets depends on what their doctor or psychologist says they need because of their disability.

After learning more about accommodations, Matt was happy to know that it is his legal right to get an accommodation. Also, he wouldn't be getting an accommodation unless Dr. Jerry felt that he needed it to reach his potential and do his very best. This made him feel better about getting accommodations.

(Scales of Justice)

(Thumbs up for legal rights to accommodations)

With help from his parents, Matt talked to the people who ran his school. His teacher, Ms. Rumsey, was in the meeting too. They all wrote a 504 plan together. Section 504 is in the Rehabilitation Act and applies to places like schools, so an accommodation plan at a school is sometimes called a "504 plan."

Matt and Ms. Rumsey talked about how to set up accommodations for tests. Miss Rumsey would work with him to set up a private place to take his tests. He would also get extra time and a computer to write out long answers.

Matt was a little scared that Miss Rumsey would think he wasn't smart, but she said there were 4 other people in Matt's class who had 504 plans. And she even had accommodations when she was in college. Miss Rumsey has ADHD which was probably why she was such an exciting teacher and knew how to keep the attention of the class.

You never know who might have a disability because many disabilities you can't see. It's almost like being in a secret club. Matt wished there was a secret handshake he could give to people to find out who else had a disability.

Luckily there was the Center for Independent Living in the city where Matt lived, so he could meet other people with disabilities.

Some people there had disabilities you couldn't
see, like Matt. And some had disabilities you could
see: like Michelle, who used a wheelchair; or Sy,
who signed because he was Deaf; and Percy, who was
blind.

Matt was so happy to find other people who also
needed accommodations. He felt like he found his
second family. A second family that included 49
million Americans! That's how many people in the
United States have a disability.

Matt and his accommodation lived happily and successfully ever after!

Of course, that was after a lot of really hard work. Matt had to advocate for himself. It also helped to have lots of supportive people around him.

Once Upon a Workbook
telling your own story

You are the star of this part of the book! Here you will take a closer look at your own disability, what accommodations help you, and what you are good at. You can write or draw your answers (just like how Dave drew the pictures for Nina's words in this book).

On this page draw a picture of yourself:

What Does It Mean to Have a Disability?

Matt had a Learning Disability. But there are lots
of different disabilities that you can get
accommodations for. These include Attention Deficit
Hyperactivity Disorder (ADHD), Aspergers,
Dysgraphia (difficulty writing), Dyscalculia
(difficulty in math), Autism, Tourette's,
Depression, and Obsessive Compulsive Disorder
(OCD), just name a few! According to the law, you
get accommodations because a disability might make
it hard to do certain things. It was important for
Matt to learn about his disability and it is
important for you to understand yours.

What is your disability (or disabilities) called?
Write or draw your answer:

Challenges I Sometimes Have

What things does your disability make challenging for you? There are boxes you can check and also a page to write or draw the difficulties you have that are not on this list.

- ☐ Reading
- ☐ Spelling
- ☐ Paying attention
- ☐ Listening to what people are saying
- ☐ Talking to people
- ☐ Understanding when someone is teasing me
- ☐ Calculating numbers
- ☐ Hand writing/Printing
- ☐ Doing math
- ☐ Understanding where things go in a room or shapes on a page
- ☐ Starting activities like homework or projects
- ☐ Takes you a little longer to learn something
- ☐ Get nervous
- ☐ Get sad
- ☐ Not always feeling good about yourself
- ☐ Tics
- ☐ Talking
- ☐ Fidgety

<u>What else? Draw or write what other difficulties</u>
<u>you have</u>:

My Accommodations

Matt received accommodations for the difficulties he had in school. Someone like Dr. Jerry will tell you what accommodations you should have to help you in school or other parts of your life (work, sports, dance class, etc...). For example, the author of this book, Nina, had accommodations in school, but she also needed to have them in other parts of her life like when she had her first job. Below is a list of accommodations. Check the accommodations that were recommended for you. If there are some that are not on this list then write or draw what them on the next page.

- ☐ Extra time on tests. I get this much more time for tests: _____

- ☐ Note-taker for classes

- ☐ Books or tests read out loud by a person or computer

- ☐ A computer, iPad, or other device to help you write assignments.

- ☐ Doing less problems in a particular subject. For example, doing every other problem in math

- ☐ Going to another room to complete tests or assignments

- ☐ Extra time to finish assignments

- ☐ Tests where you can say the answer instead of writing it

- ☐ Having an aide in school

What other accommodations were recommended for you? Write or draw them here:

I am so good at so many things!

Just because you have a disability does not mean that you are not talented or smart. People are smart in lots of different ways and can do lots of different things well. Write or draw what you are good at. This might include: art, drama, computers, science, hiking, being a good friend, making people laugh, being spiritual or participating in religion, costumes/make up, building things, working with little kids, sports, music, writing stories or poetry, or cooking.

<u>Use this page and the next page to write or draw the things that you are good at:</u>

Draw a picture of yourself asking for an accommodation from a teacher:

Cool People with Disabilities

Sometimes it can feel lonely to have a disability.
At first Matt felt the same way, but then he
learned that there were other kids in his class
that received accommodations. He also met people
who had disabilities that you could see, like Sy,
Michelle, and Percy. On these pages draw a picture
of yourself and other people you know who have
disabilities. These can be people you know in your
life or famous people.

Have fun!

It takes a lot of work to be in school, especially
if you have a disability that makes it harder. On
these pages draw or write 5 things that you like to
do. Remember to do these a lot when you are having
a difficult time in school!

Advocating for Myself!

A script is what an actor reads from when they are in a movie or play. It is important to have a script when you are asking teachers (or whoever else) for accommodations. This is a script for you to fill in so you can practice asking for an accommodation. This will help you to advocate for yourself!

I have a disability called:

_____

That means I have a difficult time doing:

_____

_____

_____

To help me I need accommodations. These accommodations are:

_____

_____

_____

_____

_____

_____

Nina G is a disability activist, humorist, and educator living in Oakland, California. She was diagnosed with a Learning Disability when she was eight years old. She also stutters. Because of her Learning Disability she never thought she would be successful in school but now she has her doctorate.

Nina would like to dedicate this book to everyone who has supported and inspired her. Especially her parents and other people who can be found in this book.

Connect with Nina online at
NinaGcomedian.com

Mean Dave is the fictional on-stage persona/character that performs stand-up comedy and loud, abrasive music for the general public.

As a young lad, lil' Mean Dave had a dream of being a cartoonist. This dream was crushed by a horrible art teacher in the 7th grade who consistently graded Dave's artwork as C or below regardless of effort, favoring high-end superficial outcomes over a child's effort and interest in the arts, namely cartooning. Mean Dave gave up his hopes yet somehow found himself accomplishing things beyond his wildest dreams as a result of this artistic disappointment. Things like playing in cool bands, making cool movies, and performing stand-up comedy, all the while still drawing cartoons for fun in related artwork and such.

Standup comedy also led Dave to meet comedian Nina G who needed an artist to illustrate her children's book about accommodations, the result of which you are holding in your hand thus breaking the evil 7th grade teacher's spell over Mean Dave and his artwork's ambitions. This project has inspired Dave to continue drawing cartoons as well and release a series of children books and graphic novels in the coming year.

Mean Dave would like to acknowledge and thank the following people in no particular order for their help and inspiration in making this possible: Mark & Rebecca Spindler, David & Vicki Gordillo, Danielle Gordillo, Dylan Wright, Shane Noniza, and intentionally lastly however, my eternal thanks goes to Nina G for asking me to participate in this project, giving me the confidence to accomplish one of my greatest childhood dreams for a worthwhile idea and cause.

19680927R10027

Made in the USA
Charleston, SC
06 June 2013